Right IDENTITY

Right IDENTITY

A GUIDE TO IDENTITY RESTORATION
FOR HEALING AND FREEDOM

LARHONDA NICOLE

Copyright © 2021 LaRhonda Nicole

Title: Right Identity
Subtitle: A Guide to Identity Restoration for Healing and Freedom
ISBN: 978-1-952327-83-4

Scripture quotations marked (NKJV) are taken from the NEW KING JAMES VERSION®. Copyright© 1982 by Thomas Nelson, Inc. Used by permission. All rights reserved.

Scripture quotations marked ESV are from the ESV® Bible (The Holy Bible, English Standard Version®), copyright © 2001 by Crossway Bibles, a publishing ministry of Good News Publishers. Used by permission. All rights reserved.

Scripture quotations marked CSB have been taken from the Christian Standard Bible®, Copyright © 2017 by Holman Bible Publishers. Used by permission. Christian Standard Bible® and CSB® are federally registered trademarks of Holman Bible Publishers.

All rights reserved. No part of this book may be reproduced or transmitted in any form or by any means without written permission from the author.

T.A.L.K. Publishing
5215 North Ironwood Road, Suite 200
Glendale, WI 53217
Myauthorlab.com

To my parents, Larry and Anna Graves

Acknowledgments

This book is dedicated to my parents, Larry and Anna Graves, who are no longer with us. I want to thank you for raising a woman who thought far beyond her years. Even though you both are not here to see my first book published, your life, both good and bad, encouraged me to grow far beyond what you both could have imagined. Thank you for the love you were able to show me, and I thank you for the teaching moments I recognized later in life. You loved the best you knew how, and now others will get to see the fruit of your coming together. I love you and miss you greatly.

To the first person who believed in me from a little girl and who inspired me to teach and cultivate a love for books and learning. From helping to set up classrooms for the new school year to receiving all the extra supplies, Mrs. Geraldine Burton truly believed in me and to this day encourages me to continue writing. Thank you for your perseverance in seeing me excel in life.

To my most dear friend, Phillip Motley, who continued to seek out my writings when I didn't have the courage to continue due to the hurt and pain behind them. You gave feedback that helped me to be creative and express myself fully. I truly appreciate you for allowing me to be me through my words and pull those things out of me that I do not take for granted.

I want to acknowledge my tribe of ladies who have kept me accountable, allowed me to cry, be vulnerable, and be my whole and authentic self with them since 2019. Latara Venise, Theresa Horne, Stacey Shaw, and Ashley Nicole, I cannot thank you enough for everything you ladies have poured into this new woman. With tears I acknowledge your hearts, your souls, and your willingness to be vessels from God. The anointing on your life is sweet and pure; anyone who receives an opportunity to work alongside you women are blessed. I am truly thankful and honored to be with you all. Without your prayers and constant reminders of the God we serve, this book would not have come to be.

    I am forever grateful.

Contents

Acknowledgments 7

Introduction: How to Use This Book 11

Chapter One: Introduction to Identity 15

Chapter Two: Let's Talk About It 28

Chapter Three: Masked Engagements Are No
    Longer Allowed 43

Chapter Four: Issues Will Come Up 59

Chapter Five: Restoration from False Identity 75

Chapter Six: Being a Good Steward of Your Restoration 85

Chapter Seven: What God Does for You in
    Recovering Your Right Identity 92

Resources 99

Introduction
How to Use This Book

Before you read this book, I would like to take a moment to set the tone and purpose for *Right Identity*. You may believe that you have read many books when it comes to the topic of identity and how we should identify ourselves. You may have read books on how Christians need to identify themselves from the world's point of view. What this book presents is a practical guide to help you understand the issues you may have when walking out the identity God has already given you.

I am not here to present a self-help guide to finding yourself in x number of days. I am only here to show you how to begin your healing journey through eliminating the unnecessary distractions we have carried most of our life which prevent us from truly knowing who we are in Christ. This is not an overnight solution. It took years to create and grow the problems we currently face. I am here to let you know that you do not have to heal or solve all your problems by yourself.

As Christians, you may have been told to go to church five days a week, hustle and grind out your salvations, or simply solve your issues on your own. Those who do not believe in God are told to follow the world's way of handling their issues, such as seeking out some form of drugs, work titles, fame, and anything that places you at the mercy of stripping away your identity. Both examples are not the way we should conduct ourselves in this life. We all at the end of the day are humans seeking acceptance, love, and respect from all, but we have never been told how to do this without sacrificing ourselves at the altars of distractions. This is where you have help in learning a new way of living.

Some may call this person an inner voice you hear when you are convicted on something. Christians call this person Holy Spirit, their Guide, Comforter, and Counselor. For the purpose of this book, I will use Holy Spirit as the name when I refer to this person. I am a believer of Jesus Christ and all that pertains to living a life based after Him.

This is not to say if you are not a Christian, you cannot take part in this book. What I am stating is that there is powerful transformation and an intimate relationship that takes place when you decide to believe that Christ is the only one that can wash your sins away and make you a new person. I am also saying that the many blessings you could receive will be limited due to you eventually having to do it on your own without God and Holy Spirit to guide you.

To get the most out of this book, it is best to do the work at the end of each chapter. By doing this, you will begin cultivating and preparing your heart for the next section as well as become practical in your healing journey. By the end of this book, you will have your own soul care plan that you can implement in your life because it was created by Holy Spirit and your willingness to change. This means you will be able to walk out your own healing according to how God has you to do. You have stayed in a place of complacency for far too long and have allowed people, places, and things to tell you who you are. How is that working for you? Are you happy? Are you comfortable?

In Matthew 11:28–thirty, *The Message* translation states:

Are you tired? Worn out? Burned out on religion? Come to me. Get away with me and you'll recover your life. I'll show you how to take a real rest. Walk with me and work with me-watch how I do it. Learn the unforced rhythms of grace. I won't lay anything heavy or ill-fitting on you. Keep company with me and you will learn to live freely and lightly.

It is not the heart of God to keep you suffering and spinning your wheels to perform for the world. That is no longer your portion in life. You are to operate in the freedom and in the will of God, which carries you through difficult challenges in life. We have become so codependent on the world and its ways that we have forgotten who created it all. We have become slaves to the creation so that we kill ourselves daily hustling and grinding for money, attention, love, and even peace.

While reading, pay attention to the areas that make you uncomfortable. I suggest making a specific journal for this. In writing down those uncomfortable moments, you will be able to discover that there are areas in your life you may need to focus more closely on, or areas you have gained are in the process of gaining victory in. The enemy is happy when he knows you are ignorant to your identity and afraid when you find revelation on who you are and whose you are. When you begin to seek the ways of healing from your roots, you bring God's glory, miracles, and love to earth. That is our goal, to make God known to others through our testimonies and victories.

I hope this begins to spark the flame for the things of God pertaining to you. As you heal, you will be the healing balm to others around you. As you walk in your right identity, you germinate the seed God planted in you to share with others. His harvest is us, and we need to be healed in order to see the kingdom come on earth as it is in heaven.

Chapter One
Introduction to Identity

If you have picked up this book, more than likely it is because there is something missing in your life. You may be a teen mom, a student, a mother of many, or a wife with none. You may be a man who is tired of feeling lost and not knowing who you really are. You may be someone looking for a way out of a job or career, a survivor of abuse, or just someone who may have seen the title and became curious. There is something all of you have in common—you are experiencing a lot of distractions.

You may be seeking freedom from life's stresses. You want freedom from the generational curses that told you this will always be your life. The masks you wear are no longer handling the attacks you have in your personal life. You are seeking freedom from the pain you can't seem to get rid of emotionally or physically. And it seems like anything you try on your own, you can't maintain anymore and need solutions quick.

This book was written from an active healing space. I continue to heal; I write and share my testimony of freedom with others because often personal struggles are not spoken of once people overcome their issues. I wrote this more so for me because I needed to see freedom daily. Before I began my journey, I was in your shoes. I was there, about to take my life, twice, and contemplating a world without my presence. I was in my dark place where I perceived no one wanted to help me or be there for me. I was in a place where the masks I wore began to suffocate me so I could not breathe. Then one day, God showed His heart for me. He showed me a new and transformed mind, full of life and a restored heart for others. This was the light I needed, but I did not know how to get up or where to start.

We have all lived a life full of masks, or the people, places and things that make us who we are from a worldly standpoint. But during my own journey, I wondered, *If God says we can have a different mindset and put on the mindset of Christ, what does that look like from a kingdom perspective?*

So, you may be wondering, *Who are we from a kingdom perspective and this new mindset?* You may ask what that even means. As you read, I will explain as well as make you think of the mindset you have so far. Is it Christlike or worldlike? God's identity versus a worldview identity. You will also learn how to challenge the identity you have grown to embrace and learn to ask Holy Spirit to begin peeling back layers of trauma, hurt, abuse, etc. so that you can see yourself the way God sees you.

What Is Identity?

Before we get started, I would like to take a moment to present a common ground for us to stand on when it comes to knowing what the term identity means. Identity is defined as the state of being exactly alike and of the set of qualities that make a person different from other people. Simply put, identity is a combination of the people, places, things, and ideas that we have placed ourselves with to state who we are. The identity you exhibit is by choice.

We can identify with a combination of ideas, places, statuses, and people groups yet truly never understand who we are. Sometimes our identity is given to us by our families. We believe that we cannot change this. Some are born into prominent families, and their identity is always being shaped by who their parents are and what they are known for. Because we have free will, we are free to choose as we get older who and what we identify with and how we represent and show up for others and ourselves.

Let's Process

Take a moment and list five things that identify you or that you identify with. There is no wrong answer. This can be written in your designated journal for this book or on the lines provided.

Write five things you identify with or that define you. Who is _____ (your name)?

_____
_____
_____
_____
_____
_____
_____

Now that you have written them out, I want you to take a moment and sit with those five things. Ask yourself, who are you without these things?

Share your feelings below. If you need more space, you are free to carry this question to your journal.

_____
_____
_____
_____
_____
_____

God had me to do this exercise to begin peeling back the layers of my perceived identity and the view I had of myself. After completing this exercise, I realized that I did not have a clue who I was outside of the people, places, and things I wrote down. It was a shocking moment to me to see that, most of my life, I had been walking around, operating, and living life with different masks on in order to create something that feeds my ego.

We as humans never truly take the time to see how identifying ourselves really benefits us. I see nature ensure it is in the right environment and place to grow and thrive. I see how different animal groups kill off those members or things that do not belong in the group. But we have the hardest time letting go of those things that are choking our identity.

We do not go in as a nurse and expect to be disregarded and seen as the bottom of the barrel. Nurses are glorified to be the next best thing to a doctor, especially since COVID. Identity is so important to us that without identity, we open ourselves us to abuse, neglect, and even death.

When we identify ourselves by a particular talent, job title, career, income level, etc., we tend to act outside and against our natural flow. Have you ever experienced a person, whom you knew closely, act totally different than what they would when it is just you and them? I will use myself as an example.

I grew up in a household where it was an unspoken rule never to speak on the addiction in my house. Many knew about my father's drug and alcohol addiction, but my mother remained quiet about it to certain people. Whenever the topic was brought up, I could see the shame on her face, but it was not mentioned verbally by her. There was always an excuse given that he was getting help or treatment for it. This taught me to put on the mask that everything was fine and to be someone I was not.

As I became an adult, I began to see those same patterns in myself. Instead of exposing the hurt and brokenness from my trauma as a child, I happily put on the mask of strong, independent woman, and eventually codependency, to deal with the hurt I was afraid to talk about. I have always been a sensitive person and wore my feelings on my sleeve, but eventually I kept those emotions in because I was taught not to express. I was taught to hide and be who they wanted me to be to them. Your identity can easily be shaped, just from the small things that were displayed to you, to survive, so next we are going to look at what false identity is.

False Identity

What is false identity? False identity is a state of being that is not genuine and upright, but has an adjusted posture made to deceive or mislead people. Having a false identity does not discriminate and care who you are. We have all experienced someone who was not being their genuine self in a situation. The person was showing another side that had not been seen by anyone. Have you seen this? Have you been this person?

Most of the time, this state of false identity can creep in when there has been something traumatic happen or a wound has occurred in any stage of your life. Some damaged people may discover that the only way to deal with this event is to pretend they are someone else or attempt to protect themselves by acting a different way. They may make up a new identity and begin to walk in it. This is where the masks come into play. It may come off as a person being very nice or very mean. It may come off as being a huge people pleaser, an avoidance type personality, or passive-aggressiveness. These particular people want to be able to communicate and have healthy relationships, but they show up in the mask that they feel best suits the gathering, the business execs, the in-laws, marriages, relationships, etc.

Let's Process

In the first writing exercise, we wrote out five things that identify us or that we identify with. Please take a moment to go back over your list. Pick three things you would leave behind if you did not have to identify yourself with them or be a part of them. You may write your response next to those three things or in a separate journal and come back for the remaining ones later.

This exercise is going to help you begin to see how easily you can be deceived and bound by your own perceived identity, especially when it is from a wound or trauma that occurred at some point in your life.

When completing this exercise a few years ago, I wanted to see what I resonated with. Someone had asked me to describe who I am and what I do. I quickly put down the most important things that made me feel good about myself. What I did not put down were the things I was ashamed to admit about myself. Now this would not be the first thing you lead off with in a conversation, but the qualities I listed were protective factors of the things I hid.

For example, I would tell people I am a nice person and really like people. Deep inside, I was a people pleaser and did not like telling people no, so I learned to love them and tolerate their negative behaviors toward me. I would also say I am a problem solver and do not like to see people stuck; I was codependent and a controller. I always wanted to know the outcome and always wanted to help you, even when I did not need to.

Some identify themselves through their current situation or circumstances. An illness can be a part of your identity, but allowing the illness to define your reasons for not changing certain behaviors is a mask. Your addiction may be part of your identity, but the reasons you started are not addressed because you do not want to deal with the pain.

You may state that you are a victim, but your self-imposed victim mentality is not addressed. The right reason is you want pity and attention for a choice you decide to keep making long after the harmful incident has happened. This may hurt, but we will need to get to the root of the situation.

When I began praying to God about starting my journey of healing, I had to brace myself for the truths that would begin to surface. I did not do this alone, and Holy Spirit was there to guide me in the ways the Lord wanted me to heal. This is what you must do in order to get to the root of the issues, the false identity. This is not to make you feel worthless or sorry for yourself but to begin to uproot the identifiers that do not serve the ultimate purpose of your existence.

Signs of a False Identity

In the medical field, when a doctor sees you for an appointment, there is this game: "Can you tell me why you are here today?" Many play this game of explaining to the doctor their current situation of why they are having certain symptoms they cannot get rid of. Some may have had heartburn for months but ignored it until it began to affect their daily life.

Going with this example, the person explains that they had a little heartburn a month ago, but recently it became unbearable to the point where they must sit up in a chair at night just to sleep. The doctor may ask what things you noticed but ignored. The person may respond by saying, at first, they had some belching, taking more anti-acids or drinking more bottles of Pepto-Bismol than usual, not able to digest certain foods, especially tomato sauce, and not feel the burn later. Because of the doctor's education and experience, they are ruling out disorders that have similar symptoms, but it must be tested with blood work, images, scans, and biopsies.

Eventually, the doctor will order blood work, scans, or images and see what the results of these symptoms could be.

Sometimes it may be a matter of diet change. Other times, it could be something more serious. In either case, the doctor had to ask what signs or symptoms caused the person to come in to see about the matter.

Often, we want to hide our symptoms of false identity. We want to cover it up, take medications, depress, suppress, drink, smoke, and eat and sex away our feelings. We decide to pick up more work or have more sex in order to not think about the problems we do not want to face. As we have all experienced, not facing the issue does not make the issue go away. It grows and festers into another issue that eventually starts to snowball into a more serious disease or condition.

We then begin to blame others for touching the topic, or wound at hand, and become resentful to others who seem to be living a life of freedom. We despise others who receive the help they need and become discontent with our life. We become desperate to heal or change our situation and put on masks to cover up the ugly wound that has now appeared.

To sum it up, having a false identity requires you to work on it by yourself only. It does not involve anyone to show you the right way to handle it. It requires all your strength and effort to make sure you look the best way possible to others, even if that means sacrificing who you really are.

Let's Process

In our next writing exercise, I want you to write down some ways you have tried to hide your emotions. This could be you saying yes, when you want to say no, due to rejection or abandonment issues, or even staying in a situation that you are afraid to leave and call it long-suffering and you're now drinking to suppress.

How do I hide my emotions?

_____
_____
_____
_____
_____
_____
_____

Our Right Identity

Now that we have a foundation of identity, false identity, and the signs and symptoms of a false identity, I want to discuss what your right identity is and consists of. Before being led on my own identity journey, I looked to the world to try and find out who I was. I was persuaded with all kinds of ideas of who I should be but later discovered that my right identity did not come from people, places, things, or ideas. It came from knowing myself through God's heart and His son Jesus.

Our right identity consists of what God has already placed in us before the foundation of the world. God already set the talents, skills, and characteristics we would need in order to live the life He called us to. There is no human that can take these away—except us if we do not accept His will for our life. Many see God as a dictator, one who already has it figured out and tells us what do to. But God is not in this business at all. He truly wants you to have the best. He is just asking us to look at who we say we are and compare it to who He says we already are.

When we are walking out our identity, God is the one who shows us what that looks like, by way of the Holy Spirit. This means we do not do it alone, no matter how tough it can be. At the same time, God also gives us free will so that we can choose what we want to do. Those who choose His will for their life prosper more. They are fulfilled and hopeful for the future. The ones who choose their own way will be limited in what they receive. You can follow the laws and principles for yourself, but without God you will not satisfy what you are truly seeking. This goes for our identity. We can choose to live out the life want, manifest, etc., or we can choose to listen to Holy Spirit and receive instructions on what God is telling us about who we are in Him. Simple and straight to the point, right? Let's see.

If you have given your life to Christ, we are now heirs to the kingdom Jesus restored back to us in His death and resurrection. We are now able to go to God in confidence and ask those things that are His will for us. We no longer seek out our identity from the world because our life was bought with a price. We no longer prove ourselves in the eyes of God. When God looks at us now, He sees Jesus because of His shed blood.

We can now walk in newness with a renewed mind and identity. This means starting today, right now, we can take hold of that gift, with no catch, and begin allowing Holy Spirit to give us directions on how begin our journey. How simple is God in this sense to allow us to come and seek without anything holding us back? But this is how we can make it harder than it needs to me.

You may be asking yourself, *What does this really mean for me and my identity?* It means you no longer hide or suppress what you have endured. You are no longer being bound to the past or present and can let go of what no longer serves you or God. Jesus has given us a chance to have relationship and intimacy with God, and it requires no religious ceremony, rules, or borders. Just you, God, and Jesus.

The reason you may not accept this truth is because the world seems to be serving you what you want and need, and you do not believe God will give you greater and better. Does a good Father not give his children good gifts? Depending on your perception of a father, you may answer no, but that is where the healing of your identity will need to begin.

You may not understand that God loving you is outside of keeping laws that put you in a place to strive for His love. You may not understand that before you were born God knew you and what you will need, but your perception of Him has been polluted by how you grew up or saw Him in the world. That is okay. We all have operated out of ignorance, but today you will begin to operate from truth.

My hope is that you will begin to see the lies in your false identity and the truth in who you really are, through the heart of God. This is where you will have to dig deep, be obedient, and begin to believe that you are needed in the kingdom of God. Your life is more precious than you believe, and your experiences and stories will truly mark you as a child of God.

Our right identity is in the work Jesus did to restore our relationship. Just take inventory of your life and look at what the Bible says about your identity. No human has the manual to your life, but God does, and as the manufacturer of life He can clearly tell you who you are.

If you are unsure if you can even hear God, begin to pray and ask God the hard questions you may have. This is the time to begin to reconnect with Holy Spirit. Holy Spirit is that voice that calls you to correction in love and will tell you about the things on God's heart for you. During my journey, I had to learn to be still and listen for the voice of God to calm my anxious thoughts, and to clearly give direction in my next steps. This did not happen overnight. Just like any new routine or skill, it takes time and consistently showing up to hear the heart of God.

Let's Process

In this exercise, I want you to take some time to write out all your worries and frustrations and empty yourself of all things that you have been holding on to for so long with a closed fist. Allow your heart to open and allow them to flow on paper.

As a reminder, those people, places and things you can no longer control, allow the emotions, hurts and pains of them begin to flow in your personal journal or this space. This is the time to unload without judgment or restraints.

Write or draw as you experience the following: emptying myself.

_____
_____
_____
_____
_____
_____
_____
_____
_____
_____
_____
_____
_____
_____
_____
_____
_____
_____
_____
_____

What is Holy Spirit Saying to You?

In your journal, begin writing down what Holy Spirit is truly saying to you when it comes to your issues, wounds, and traumas that keep you stuck, hiding, or not moving in obedience. Holy Spirit is not there to condemn you or even make the situation worse. That is what Satan does to distract and take us off track from where God has us on. By making a journal, you are then able to go back and see progress, as well as how God pulls you out of torment.

_____

_____

_____

_____

_____

_____

_____

_____

_____

_____

_____

_____

_____

_____

_____

_____

_____

_____

_____

Chapter Two
Let's Talk About It

As we begin to unfold what has caused us to hide or cover up our identity, we need to discuss what brought us to this point of seeking healing and freedom. For me, it was discovering I was codependent and that my marriage was not one God would have for me.

My codependency was rooted in my dad's drug and alcohol addiction as well as my mama's constant concern and worry for him. I did not know I had a real issue until I entered school for my degree in social work. That was where my awareness of the term *healing* (beyond the physical) started. But my healing journey would not begin just yet.

My teachers in my social work program pushed me to dig deep into my past with different assignments. Before starting school, I had never been to therapy. The only people receiving therapy in our house were my brother and dad, whenever he decided to go. I was not aware of how much healing needed to take place until one day during an assignment when we had to write about our life. I realized I had a lot to say about my home life.

I was very emotional and could hardly maintain my feelings as I wrote the paper. At that time, I had never shared what my home life was like. It all came out in anger. My mask of independence and holding it all together for everyone had begun to crack. I realized in that one assignment that God was getting my attention.

As the Band-Aid on my heart began to come off, I began to see the wounds and traumas I had pent up over the years. I had begun to feel more ashamed of the sexual abuse I experienced. I began to realize I had stuffed anger I felt toward my parents for not protecting me and for when I explained what happened when I was molested. I began to feel the sting of the environments I had placed myself in when I was promiscuous and drunk and how I used them to not think about my past. This was uncomfortable because I was taught to honor my parents.

I was breaking down and could no longer hold it together for myself. The anger began to come out in my current relationships with my family and friends, and I just wanted to isolate. I avoided a lot of people during that time; I did not want to be around anyone who cared for me, due to fear of hurting them.

Remember how I stated that God had my attention? Through my assignments, God had provided therapy sessions for me. This allowed me to be more open and to express my thoughts, feelings, and emotions that had been suppressed for years. I began to discover that my false identity was no longer holding me up anymore, and I had to do something about it.

At the time, I was unaware of how Holy Spirit was working in me until one night I heard a teaching about Holy Spirit. I attended a Christian college, and we were required to take Old Testament and New Testament. One day, the professor taught on the Holy Spirit when we discussed Jesus leaving us a Comforter. After his classes I began reading more about Holy Spirit and how He would operate in the lives of all believers. I began to make sense of how vital Holy Spirit is to me and began to put into practice a dependence on Him. This was hard for me because growing up, I had learned that Holy Spirit was only a tongue spoken. Yes, speaking in tongues is not the only evidence of the Holy Spirit operating in your life. (We will save that for another book.)

Through my own curiosity about Holy Spirit, I realized there was something true to discover about how God communicates with us. I realized Holy Spirit brought correction in kindness and helped me to see solutions in people, places, things, and ideas. Holy Spirit guides and directs us but does not force His way on us. As I began to develop this relationship more and more, I soon saw the change God was showing me through my time receiving my degree. Little did I know that soon, Holy Spirit was going to be doing more than speaking to me.

Did this heal me and change me? It was a start, but I did not fully immerse myself into the process due to lack of understanding and still having a religious mindset of who God really is. This was only the start. I shared my beginning, so you are aware that not everyone becomes healed on the first try. God created an opportunity for me to walk through a door I had never experienced, and it began a journey I will never forget. Maybe your start began with a spark such as mine, but now, that spark will become a fire that will burn for God more than before, once you fully surrender.

Let's Process

Have you had a burning bush moment in your life that stopped you in your tracks? Was there a time God was trying to get your attention about who you are, but you avoided the opportunity? Take a day or two write out that moment. Write a letter to yourself explaining what happened that made you think twice about you, your existence, etc. I want to jog your memory of the time God tried to capture your attention, but maybe you missed it. This will be done on a separate sheet.

What is Your Trauma Wound?

What is a trauma wound? Well, let's define trauma. Trauma is defined as a deeply distressing or disturbing experience. The word *trauma*, in Greek, comes from the root word *wound*. Anyone who has been identified as going through trauma has endured a wound, whether it is physical or emotional or both. Some are not able to express those wounds due to the depth of the wound and, therefore, ignore the importance of healing it. Due to the pain, some refuse to uncover it. Wounds can range from any age, size, or effect on the person's life, but one common denominator is that we all try to fix it on our own, in the beginning.

As a nurse, I can care for wounds once the doctor has diagnosed it and has been able to create a plan of care for it. Doctors are trained to have a keen eye for all wounds, ranging from what type of wound and where it began, as well as what may happen if not treated. The mistake we make sometimes in diagnosing our own wound is that we believe no one understands our pain; therefore, we use various unnecessary treatments and solutions to cover up these deeply infected wounds instead of getting to the root cause of it. This leads to the very cause of infections.

Sometimes the infections are only skin deep, but some can go to the bone. We may believe our trauma wounds are not affecting our present life. Once the mask and the makeshift bandages we created begin to fall away, we realize that we cannot uphold our own healing without the help and guidance of Holy Spirit and God.

Let's Process

In the space below, write down any trauma wounds you have had over the years, even as far back as childhood, that you have not forgiven the person for or that still haunt you till this day. No wound is too big or too small or insignificant. This is another unloading moment that will need to take place. You do not have to fill all spaces, but if you do, that is okay as well.

_____
_____
_____
_____
_____
_____
_____
_____
_____
_____
_____
_____
_____
_____
_____
_____
_____
_____
_____
_____
_____

Triggers

Now that we have laid our issues and trauma wounds down, this is the brave moment we take to make a choice to heal. They create a care plan and make sure to add preventive measures so that the injury does not happen again. They also must tell you to stay away from certain things so that you do not reinjure, or trigger, the wound. The doctor is making sure you do not have any triggers to sabotage your healing. So let's define triggers.

The triggers we have are constant reminders of the trauma wounds. Triggers can be defined as automatic negative responses to common emotions, responses, or situations in our life. To reiterate, these can be people, places, things, or even ideas that are normal, but our experiences and wounds make us react as though we are in danger and go into survival mode.

Often these are normal outside external factors that are harmless. These may set off triggers that will give the subconscious permission to act and perceive a situation different than what is being presented. This different reaction results in issues and lack of accountability and responsibility, which may damage relationships, especially where the other person is unaware of the abuse or the level of trauma that was experienced.

The partner can simply cook a meal, and the smell triggers their partner. An argument or wrong perception comes out, harming the unsuspecting person. Is that fair? Is that how you would want to continue to live life? No one wants to always live life on the edge.

Let me give you an example. I was a child of an alcoholic and drug-addicted father; his drug of choice was crack cocaine. I have seen him inject with his needles, as well as smoke it. Just the smell of metal can send me back to my emotions associated with him getting high. Those included anger, rage, and sadness because once he was high, I knew it was going to be a long day or night at the house.

There can also be physical responses. For me, my heart would race when I saw him use the drug, because I knew it was going to also mean my mother was going to be verbally or physically abused. Up until my midtwenties when I was out on my own, I had a habit of checking the back of spoons for burn marks because my mother told us to always throw them away if we ever saw them. My dad used them sometimes to cook his drug. But I had to realize that if I did smell it or saw a burned spoon, I was not in that place of insecurity anymore. That took years of work, but it was powerful to know that it was not normal for those things to occur.

The same is true for you. If you have triggers that continue to affect your present moment, seeking therapy and asking Holy Spirit how to resolve the feelings and emotions that come up will truly help you overcome and heal. Always remember that triggers were our past response to dangerous situations, not our present moment.

Let's Process

In the space below or in your journal, write down your triggers and why they are triggers to you. I would also like for you to write out how these triggers have affected you in your daily life. What has it stopped you from doing or experiencing? You can make this a list for each trigger you list.

Triggers

For this exercise, identify three to five triggers and write about them on the lines provided or in a separate journal. Here are questions to consider:

1. What are my triggers?

2. Why are these my triggers?

3. How have these triggers affected my life?

4. What has it stopped me from doing or experiencing in life?

Trigger #1

_____
_____
_____
_____
_____
_____

Trigger #2

_____
_____
_____
_____
_____
_____

Trigger #3

_____
_____
_____
_____
_____
_____

Trigger #4

_____
_____
_____
_____
_____
_____

Trigger #5

_____
_____
_____
_____
_____
_____

Unhealthy Coping Mechanisms

Unhealthy coping mechanisms are habits that do not bring about healthy actions or results. As we begin to uncover triggers and masks we wear to cope with life, we also begin to see that we have produced bad habits that do not benefit our overall well-being. Using the example of wound care, we ask our patients to begin drinking more water instead of soda or sugary drinks. This is to aid in healing and reduce the amount of processed sugar in the system, giving the body more room to heal than fight off increased sugar levels.

Our patients are not happy about this, but we must educate them on the importance of producing a healthy environment for healing on the inside. Do you have a healthy environment for healing inside you?

As I began to walk through my journey of Holy Spirit uncovering people, places, and bad habits that were not benefiting me, I did not like it. I knew the Band-Aid was being removed, and I had to begin working through the pain. Not having a drink when I was depressed or upset, not seeking sex when I really wanted companionship, because I knew men were able to give that when sex was on the table—these things I could no longer do.

I had to be okay being alone when I wanted sex. I had to okay with being rejected by people that I believed had my best interest when I told them of what I was going through. It was all necessary, but it began to uncover deeply rooted issues I had not begun to even touch.

The unhealthy coping mechanisms can also be the masks you use to cover up to show up. You may drink socially to fit in when you really do not want a drink. You may cuss or gossip in order to be relevant in a conversation you do not even want to be a part of. You may change your identity to fit the very people who are using you due to what and who you identify with.

All these things are unhealthy because they stifle the truth about you. When you remove all these factors and lie open and naked, you cannot hide the scars anymore. Everything is out in the open to be dealt with, and God is your ultimate covering in not exposing you to any more harm once you are ready.

Let's Process

In the space below, list unhealthy coping mechanisms you have used or currently use to keep your pain or embarrassment, at a level you have been able to control thus far. These do not have to be substances, but they can be behaviors that have served you up until this point.

Unhealthy Coping Mechanisms

1. _____
2. _____
3. _____
4. _____
5. _____
6. _____
7. _____
8. _____
9. _____
10. _____

False Beliefs

False beliefs are a gateway to remaining stuck in the mask you created to cover your pain. If you believe you are not to receive God's best for you, then you will not be able to fully uncover those issues that you remain in. Our thought life is powerful, and if we are not addressing and uncovering the very things that keep us away from God, we will continue to play victim and believe life is unfair. This is not God's best for you.

As we begin to heal, our mentality changes from believing we are victims of our circumstances to a mindset that takes accountability and responsibility for our actions. I was told by my mentor once I started working with her on my healing that *I have a choice*. That was the most powerful statement I received in my journey.

Most of my life, I played the victim, knowing I did not take accountability for my part in the cycle of abuse or trauma. But then, I began to heal and realized I could no longer play that same sad song in my head anymore. Notice I did not say when I got older but *when I began to heal*. Just because you are fifty or over doesn't mean you are healed. There are generations of people still carrying old wounds who refuse to uncover and heal from them. This is because the thoughts we believe are what come to be.

You may hear a lot of people tell you, you can create whatever reality you believe. In some ways this is right, but only if it is in line with God's will for your life. It is funny to hear that statement, but none of those same people talk about healing from the past. They always want to create but never heal. You will hear them use your pain or wounds to get what they need from you. This is not biblical or right. Many people state that their misery is their ministry. I don't know about you, but I do not want someone's misery preaching or ministering to me. We must see and hear what others are saying because we will become consumers of the ideas of the world and believe God is in it.

God does not honor anyone staying in their misery. He loves us too much to want us to stay there. God tells us to rise above it all by following the ways of Jesus. He does not pride himself on His children being in their heads. He is always encouraging us to face our wounds. He reminds us in His Word that we are His children, and He gives us good gifts. When He created the world, He said it was good. When He made man and woman, He said they were good.

Our beliefs and what we believe to be right is most of the time perverted. The meaning of the word *perverted* simply means distorted. There is a pattern of the world many have followed, including myself. We are told in order to be successful, we must sacrifice our family, and the world applauds; that in order to rise above the ranks in anything, we must sacrifice our values and God to get there. I say this because in any situation where your identity is compromised, there is a certain belief system you must subscribe to in order to maintain your belief in it.

A false belief system always sacrifices your values, especially when your values are rooted in God's way for your life. For example, when you work long shifts but say you value your family, your values are dismissed. When you want a healthy sex life from your husband or wife but watch porn daily, you sacrifice the good thing God has given you. Instead of us dealing with these beliefs, we cover them up in our careers, places, people, etc. that do not matter.

Let's Process

In the space below, I want you to take some time to write down the false beliefs you have held that contributed to where you are currently. It does not matter how big or small these beliefs are, but that they are beliefs you have carried for a while.

LET'S TALK ABOUT IT

What is Holy Spirit speaking to you?

In this space, journal about what you have learned, as well as what Holy Spirit has been speaking to you about you after reading this chapter. If there are any solutions that come to mind, write them down, even if it does not make sense. Remember that the healing that is to take place is by the choice you make now.

_____
_____
_____
_____
_____
_____
_____
_____
_____
_____
_____
_____
_____
_____
_____
_____
_____
_____
_____
_____

Chapter Three
Masked Engagements Are No Longer Allowed

As I began to walk in this new life of following my right identity, I realized things I was involved in or wanted to do no longer were pleasing to me. I have my degree in social work and nursing and had decided to open a home care business in 2018, because I felt this would put money in my pockets due to my passion for those who are vulnerable. I had been a caregiver to my parents for many years, and having this business, I thought, was going to be the ultimate dedication to my service as a caregiver. So I created the plan, saved the money, and worked to get the foundation going but realized I was doing everything on my own. I was tired, burned out, and in compassion fatigue.

After getting to the point where I was worn out with hiring and marketing this business, I had a moment where I was upset. I was doing what was right, but it was not prospering. I finally had to admit that I had not truly sought God for the vision of this business—or even if this was the business He wanted me to have. After allowing myself to have a pity party, I let it go in May 2020. Before 2020, the desire to close was already there, but COVID forced my hand to shut it down because no one was allowing anyone into their home.

After making the decision to close the business during COVID, I went into a short-lived depression state that had me questioning what I am really placed on this earth to do. What I learned in that season was that I lacked patience and trust in God and God's provision. I am not saying having a home care business is bad, but it was not what God had for me. When I began to surrender all my desires, wants, and needs, I finally understood that God is not taking anything good away from me. God needed me to work on my heart and character so that I could accept His best for me.

I saw that everything I believed about myself had been put into a business, a marriage, and a false identity, and I gave it to others like a business card. I was already working with a mentor at that time, and God showed me that I needed to keep learning and listening to what she had to say because it was setting me free.

The masks were coming off because I decided to take them off. I was able to see when I wanted to put on a mask and, most importantly, the reasons why. In the process, I learned a lot about my true identity. I realized I did not like the work of caregiving. This took me by surprise! I realized I did not like telling others what to do; I realized I had control issues and felt a need to tell others what to do. Eventually, that realization led to me not wanting to control people any longer. In that moment, God showed me my true identity and how He wanted me to show up.

The truth was that I cared enough to not see people suffer. Instead of going in to save them from their choices or be a martyr for the choices they made on their own, I was now operating from a place of kindness and love for the person. I was now wanting them to hear from God instead of me being their god. And if God called me to help them, I would step in at that time if I choose to, but no longer out of obligation. This new vision God has for me changed my life and the trajectory it was going.

The masks of rejection, abandonment, not feeling loved or worthy of love, and many more are the masks I no longer need to wear. Today I am still throwing away masks because my healing is allowing me to see clearly that they are no longer needed for me to survive. I need to breathe in order to thrive. Mask engagement is no longer my cup, and I do not attempt to reach for them because Holy Spirit has given me tools to use and strategy on how to deal with the reasons and wounds behind the mask.

Let's Process

Using your journal or this space, begin to answer these questions.

1. What masks are you wearing?

   _____
   _____
   _____

2. What do those masks look like?

   _____
   _____
   _____

3. How do you show up without your masks?

   _____
   _____
   _____

After answering these questions, ask Holy Spirit how you begin to take these masks off for good. Remember, this is not an overnight process. You have been creating a habit of putting these masks on and now, through obedience, you will be able to remove them permanently.

Accountability and Responsibility

The twins to a better and more abundant life are accountability and responsibility. Accountability is defined as taking and accepting responsibility for an act you committed. Responsibility is when you accept the results of the action you took. You may ask, *Why are these two words important?* They are essential in healing as well as moving forward from trauma wounds. Going back to those who identify as victims of their circumstances, we see that accountability and responsibility were absent from their life.

When we begin to use these words, the decisions we make have a different weight to them. No one makes an adult do something they do not want to do. Daily we make choices to do good or bad, to protect and survive. To say you are a victim means you are telling the story that you had no control over what you decided to do. Now, this does not go for situations where you were forced and your life was in danger of being taken. Those are situations where you had no control because someone had presumed power to take your life. I am referring to situations where you decided to stay in a known environment that was not safe or suitable for life. If you are in a situation and there is a choice to be made, you are responsible and accountable to yourself and whoever else may be in your care.

The best example of accountability and responsibility is when people mention that God allows all bad things to happen. God acknowledges that the world is full of sin. He takes responsibility and accountability for it all. He also mentions how He has given others free will to choose. That means He is aware people are free to make their choices. He also mentions that He sent Jesus to be the living sacrifice. Jesus took the fall for all of us who make the wrong choices within our free will. We fail to see that God does not come down and cause sin; we are living, breathing, and acting in sin, but we do not want to take responsibility for our actions in them.

We tend to blame others and place the responsibility on them because we refuse to see the part we played in it. Imagine what would happen if we all decided to make choices that were healthy and not from a place of desperation, fear, worry, etc. Our lives may have turned out different. I know mine would have, but now we are moving forward in the grace we have been given.

When we are hurt, we make choices out of pain and wanting to end the suffering. When those wounds create life decisions, wrong thinking, and unbreathable masks, the world tends to celebrate this and allow us to live in a state of distorted thinking, or what the medical professionals called mental illness and diseases.

Life does not have to be the sum of all your mistakes and hurt. We can turn that all around today by allowing God to come in and love us where we are. I had to understand clearly that He does not want us to remain in that state. Remaining in this state means you have not let go of control for the outcome of your life. You keep holding on when it is time to let go. God is telling you to let go and make that exchange, His will for your life versus your will for your life. Which one will you choose today?

How God Sees You

God sees you. Yes! Even in your fetal position on the floor, no make-up, wigs, weaves, or lashes, just nothing. He sees you more clearly than you see yourself, and He knows what you need. I need you all to take a moment and inhale that statement.

God sees you more clearly than you see yourself, and He knows what you need.

Who do you know in your life, besides a close loved one or friend, who knows you intimately? Who knows you so intimately that they can detect anything wrong in how you said a certain word? God knows us and He sees us. God knows you when you have a distorted view of yourself. God knows and can speak to that hurt to remove it from you if you allow.

God sees past the substances you put into your body to stop the pain, even the injections and fillers use to keep yourself looking youthful. You see, abuse, rejection, abandonment, longing to be attached to your biological parents, the need of the sweet touch of someone who has passed away, the hopeful kiss from a loved one you missed—God sees that, too, and He can comfort you in those moments, if you allow Him to.

When you begin to become vulnerable and allow the shame and guilt to fall, you will begin to see that God is more than an invisible force working on your behalf in your life. You begin to see God as the ultimate source of life, like water and air. God is constantly reminding us of who we are to Him because we are His example of His love and grace on our life. We may not understand why He loves us. I still wrestle with the idea as I write, but I know I can count on His love daily and allow the wrestling to stop.

Despite feeling the sense of helplessness and defeat, God says you are a new creature because of the work Jesus did. I believe Jesus came to restore the relationship we had with God, and because of his death, burial of our sins, and resurrection, I am redeemed! Jesus reconciled the relationship we were not deserving of. We are made new because of Jesus's sacrifice. Now, when God sees you and me, He sees Jesus, and every day I am being molded into His image by choice, because I understand that Jesus paid it all.

God says we are righteous and holy because we willingly chose to put on the right identity. We choose daily to follow the ways of Christ and not be shaken by the world's demands to be perfect. There is a difference. We are no longer bound, and we can be set free from those chains. You also can be set free if you willingly deny the chains that keep you in pain. Our wounds and traumas keep us in a perpetual state of hurt and fear because we have not learned to lean in. But I am telling you right now, in order to be healed, in order to move in freedom, release the chains you have kept! It is time to embrace what God says about you versus was the enemy says about you.

God says, *You have been saved by grace, my daughter and son*. This means that you did not have to do anything to earn this grace that is given to you. You believed in Jesus and the work He did on our behalf. No one can take credit for what God has given. You do not have to perform or be something you are not in order to gain it. Just as a gift is given without expectations, this new life we have been called to requires nothing but us walking closely with God and listening to His voice in obedience.

God says you are designed for good works, and these works were prepared before the foundations of this earth. Just think for a second, when the issues of life are laid at the feet of Jesus, can you imagine knowing that you have exchanged the heaviness of this world's troubles for the gifts God already created for you to have? Because before we had wounds, masks, expectations, etc., we were already given good gifts. God just wants us to take on the right identity to accept them. Therefore, having the right identity will keep you from the enemy's tactics and traps we all will face while here on earth. It does not mean we won't face anything hard, but it means we do not have to face it alone.

Let's Process

In your journal or the space below, I want you to write out the chains, trauma, pain, wounds, etc. that need to be released right now. Even with your tears, I need you to begin to write what you need to let go. As you allow the tears to fall, as you release the heaviness of the pain you feel in your throat, chest, legs, etc., release and write what Holy Spirit is saying to you now.

Is it shame that needs to be released? Guilt over the mistakes from last night? These issues could have happened days ago, hours ago, decades ago—write it. As God begins working on you, remember that these things may have taken years away, but God says we are allowing these things to be released today.

Write out the chains, trauma, pain, wounds, etc. that need to be released.

_____
_____
_____
_____
_____
_____
_____
_____
_____
_____
_____
_____
_____
_____
_____
_____
_____

Intimacy with God

God created us to be seeds to others. What does that mean? It means a farmer does not plant bad seeds and expect a good harvest. It means that God did not create us just to be bad fruit for others. Every one of us—yes, even the person you do not like—is one of God's seed, sown into this earth to multiply and harvest what is needed for His sons and daughters.

God's way of defeating the enemy was not through physical war, but spiritually. God's chess move was to allow the seed to know its right identity from the very beginning so that it would not be confused in the world once it got here. God put in the seed all it needed to live on earth and thrive even in the harshest condition. God knew what your neighbor would need way before you were created and then created you to give the very thing they needed at the right place and time.

Take a moment and think how important lemon trees are to apple trees. There are different varieties of apples today. They all start from a seed that looks similar. You never think what kind of apple tree it will be, unless you specifically removed a seed from a package that had the name of the apple on it. You may think, *I want an apple that is good for making an apple pie*. And God has already created such an apple. You may be in the mood for a tart apple, so God created Granny Smiths. But one day, someone needed a way to preserve these apples, and one way of saving them is in lemon juice.

Now God had thought this out way in advance and included lemons in His catalog of fruit just so someone can discover that it helps with keeping things fresh longer. How amazing is it that one of the qualities God wanted the lemon tree to have is preservation? If you take the time to google, lemons are used for a variety of things, but its purpose all started before the foundation of the world, and God saw the need well in advance that we would be preserving food with lemons. The key to knowing this from a human perspective was through intimacy in finding out the qualities of the apple, the qualities of the lemon, and pulling out the quality that was suited for preservation.

Just like you; God saw a need from someone, so He created you. Maybe your need in the earth comes from how you talk to others. Maybe how you are so helpful and giving and how you nurture people back from dark places. Maybe it is the very thing you dislike about yourself, and God has already told you that He has need of you. When we shed off all the things the world has placed on us and we allow ourselves to truly show up as God has created us, we are powerful. The things God is wanting to exchange with you are the things God can use to being others back to Him, but it requires intimacy with God in order to know His heart.

You are more powerful when you shed layers of disappointment, hurt, anger, unforgiveness, etc. The world says these things are perceived as weakness or that they are seen as small things. I am here to say God does nothing small. I am here to remind you that the enemy cannot create but can only imitate what God has already done naturally and with ease.

The space you create when you let go of all the things that have defined you in this world is a space of intimacy with God. God can only move in places that allow His spirit to flow freely. When we begin to come to God and express our deepest hurts, we allow God to open spaces in us we would have never opened to another person. Even in this moment, I am allowing God to go deep within me to heal wounds and Holy Spirit can move freely within. When we allow this to happen, things will change.

Our intimacy creates space to say, *I am wrong*. It creates an atmosphere that tells God yes and allows Him to take priority. We begin to depend on His every Word and stand firm on it. We allow our past person, who was in survival mode, to be at peace and allow Christ to show up in our life. We are never the same. I never thought in a million years, I would be opening myself up to hundreds of people daily through my videos and conversations.

Wounds from my mother and father keep me in tears, but the difference is that I can now confidently go to God and ask Him how to handle them. I now see men and women as human beings that need a Savior versus my old way of being self-righteous and asking silly questions of how God can allow hurt. I can now say no to people and understand my no is valid. I can now stand and say *Jesus is my Lord and Savior* and not feel judged because of my beliefs. I feel freedom, but it only came after I began to become intimate with God's heart and naked before Him.

There has been a level of vulnerability I have never experienced with a human being. Just being in His presence changed my approach. I am no longer an orphan, abandoned or rejected. I am accepted, loved, and cared for by God daily. This can be your cup as well. Have you reached this level of vulnerability with God? Have you truly revealed all there is about you to Him? Have you decided I am going to let it all out and trust God with my wounds, false beliefs, upsets, disappointments, etc. and give Him everything so that I can move in freedom from the chains of this world?

Let's Process

Write in your journal or in the space below, at what level of intimacy are you with God? Explain your level. After writing, begin to ask Holy Spirit, How can I increase my level of intimacy?

_____
_____
_____
_____
_____

RIGHT IDENTITY

Vulnerability

Vulnerability is defined by *Oxford Languages* on Google as "the quality or state of being exposed to the possibility of being attacked or harmed, either physically or emotionally." When we are vulnerable in the world's sense, it is seen as being placed in danger due to your race, color, age, status, etc. We tend to be on guard and not allow others into our worlds. We see danger around every corner, yet we are never equipped to deal with being vulnerable.

We are not taught in school how to have a healthy level of vulnerability because it is perceived as weakness rather than strength. God spoke to me about my level of vulnerability and stated I was not vulnerable at all with Him. I work as a social worker and a nurse, and there is a level of vulnerability you need in order to serve properly. But I covered it up by wearing my mask of being stoic. I wanted the families to have their moments while I stood back holding tears or fear for their loved ones. Some would ask me how I manage not to express emotions, and I would tell them that it is about their family, not my feelings. I had to hold it in because I would come apart and did not want them seeing me in this way.

Before I became a nurse, I saw this in other nurses. They expressed no emotions. The ones that did, we looked at as weak. We would ask why they were crying and not us. Little did I know that a person who allows that moment to be expressed amid death or sorrow is a strong person, because it takes a level of vulnerability to shed emotions for someone you may not know a lot about or not know at all. When I became a nurse, I carried those emotions I wanted to express, and sometimes I did not deal with it until 2019, when I had my breakthrough moment. Here is a vulnerable yet powerful moment I want to share with you all that made me realize, at that time, I was tired and couldn't hold on to the masks I wore.

After my mother passed in 2016, I remember wanting to be near her so bad. I wanted to feel her and smell her again. But I could not express this because there was a level of vulnerability I had not expressed to any of my family who were sitting near her bed before she passed away. In 2019, I had a breaking moment where I woke up one Sunday morning with an extreme urge to push out all my emotions. I found myself on my bathroom floor, screaming out to God how much I wanted my mother again.

At the time, my husband and my son were out of town. I knew they would not be back, so I decided to have some time to myself. The moment I was about to experience was like nothing I had ever experienced in my life, but God allowed it to happen for a reason. I was in my bathroom about to take a bath, and suddenly, an overwhelming flood of emotions came from out of nowhere it seemed.

I cried and literally was in a pool of tears on my cold bathroom floor. I could not stop crying, even if I wanted to. I remember still having water in the tub and how I had my hands in the water grabbing at it just to feel something. *I need to mourn* was what I kept thinking, but I found it strange later that I was trying to control that moment. I realized I had not mourned my mother's death, and I had all these pent-up emotions in me. I remember yelling out loud till my voice was hoarse and yelling more.

After I gathered my composure, I began to sit in silence on my bathroom floor against the sink, naked. I had no reserves about myself. I did not care if they found me in the bathroom that way. I didn't care that my water was cold. All I knew in that moment was that God allowed me to weep profusely at His feet for my mother and for myself. He came and allowed me to not be strong anymore, and I could feel his presence covering me in my moment of vulnerability. I could not imagine a more peaceful moment in my life when I let go of the perception of weakness.

Now, I would like to say that I now cry at the drop of a dime. At times there can be a struggle with allowing the tears to flow and holding back, but I know God made tears and it is okay to cry. There are times I know I do not need to become unhinged, and God guides those moments and creates safe spaces and places to flow. Even with my friends, now I can allow myself to feel my emotions and be in a vulnerable space with them because I know God allowed that moment to occur in my life.

Let's Process

In the space below, write out the beliefs you have around vulnerability. How do you show up when you need to be vulnerable? In what areas of your life are you not vulnerable with God and why?

_____
_____
_____
_____
_____
_____
_____
_____
_____
_____
_____
_____
_____
_____
_____

What is Holy Spirit Speaking to You?

In this space, journal about what you have learned in this chapter, as well as what Holy Spirit has been speaking to you about you and any changes that need to take place today. If there are any solutions that come to mind, write them down, even if it does not make sense. Remember that the healing that is to take place is by the choice you make now, and it may not be as hard as you have believed.

_____
_____
_____
_____
_____
_____
_____
_____
_____
_____
_____
_____
_____
_____
_____
_____
_____
_____
_____

Chapter Four
Issues Will Come Up

As you heal, it is inevitable that issues of your life will come up. Life does not stop or place everything on hold while you are recovering. Just as when you are finally in your hospital room after surgery, the nurse is given a care plan to follow to make sure this infection, sickness, etc. does not happen again. This section I will discuss the soul care plan you and Holy Spirit will create together to ensure you will not relapse or pause in your restoration process.

I am asking you to partner with Holy Spirit, if you have not already, because Holy Spirit is where there are clear, simple instructions from the heart of God. These instructions are not polluted with the world's ways of healing, but from heaven above. God knows your heart. God understands your pain. Who else would be perfect to receive Holy Spirit-led healing from other than from the manufacturer? When there is something wrong with our car and it still has warranty on it, we do not take it to some mechanic shop, we take it back to the dealer who specializes in that car and has parts ready to go.

As we have gone through the signs and symptoms of false identity, what has not worked for you, and the basic foundations of restoring your identity, I want to discuss your care plan. I like to call it your *soul care plan*. You may ask, *What is a soul care plan?* A soul care plan is a plan designed by you and Holy Spirit to create a more functional space in your life that includes your mind, body and spirit health.

This is not a new concept. This has been practiced for many centuries and recently has been creeping its way into other practices that do not involve Holy Spirit. For example, Jesus practiced soul care by getting away from the crowds after hours of giving the message. Jesus went and prayed to His Father when necessary. Jesus was found in the temple, as a young kid, receiving the teachings of His Father. He knew where He needed to be because He knew His identity rested on how He cared for himself and his needs. We do not do this often.

We believe in self-care, which is not a bad thing. It is included in soul care, but I am referring to those essential needs that no one knows about us. For example, I truly desire peace in my home, on my job, and any place I go, so I created boundaries and time frames when people can and cannot reach out to me. When I am at work, I take my lunch breaks away from everyone and do not believe in a working lunch break. If I need to, I will clock out and take a lunch and go to my car to relax.

This is how important peace is to me. I do not allow anyone in my home after a certain time. If you are a gossiper, I do not allow you in my home because I do not gossip. This restriction aligns with my values and priorities. As a last example, my son likes spending quality time with me. Family is in my list of priorities, so every Wednesday night between five and nine p.m., we will pick a movie to watch. Those things are included in my soul care plan.

This type of plan allows space for you to be who you are and create more room for God's yes and respect your needs as well. In the next few sections, you will create a soul care plan based on what you know is important to you. Do not worry. This is not a section to be rushed and may take a few days, but do not dwell on what you are being told and what comes up. If you do not understand or are uncomfortable about it, write it down and take it in prayer to receive clarity on the issues.

Values and Priorities

For those who rise in the morning and just go, go, go without a plan, what are your priorities? For those who have no plan for the day and allow anything and everything to happen, what are your values? As one who knows all too well these patterns and routines I had created over the years, I realized I had a choice in deciding how my day was going to go. For example, I knew each day I had to work and all my tasks and responsibilities for the job I was performing. I knew that if I did not get those things done, it would end up going to the next person who was coming on shift. Depending on who it was, I wanted to make sure I had all my ducks in a row, or I would be fussed at during report.

In my personal life, I did not have that same mindset. I just went about my day, not caring about what I really had to do and allowing tasks to pile up into the next day. When the next day came, I would rob myself of joy because I had not completed my tasks from the previous day. I was continuing to discount my time and not be intentional about it. So, what happened? Depression, anxiety, procrastination, and guilt began to build up till I felt the world crashing in on me. I had no values or priorities set in place for my own life.

You may be wondering, *What does this have to do with me and my identity?* It has everything to do with it. You see, when we do not place value and priority over the things that God has told us about ourselves—the things that make us thrive in Him, be productive, or give us joy—we discount our time with others and, most importantly, ourselves. For example, my peace is important to me. If I did not value it, I would not make time for it. So, when I would want to go to bed in peace, but my phone rings and it's a sibling or a friend of mine, I would pick up and talk. That led to lack of sleep, and then I am cranky in the morning and trying to spend time getting myself together with only three hours of sleep.

That then leads to me not having time for other things I value, such as time with my son, because I am mad at my siblings or friends for keeping me on the phone all night, and I am wasting time in the morning trying to get myself together. Just in that sentence it seems so draining, but that is what we do when we cannot point out what we value the most and prioritize those in our life. Because I was able to take the time to sit and really narrow down my values, I felt more in control of my life than in previous times. I felt responsible for the time I was stewarding over versus blaming others for wasting it. I value my time more, and I still trip up when I allow people to take it, or I spend too much time procrastinating.

Let's Process

In the space below or in your journal, list ten things you value in your life. These are values that you must have in order to have a productive day as well as those things that give you control over your life. (If you are unsure of what values are or what they look like, do a search on "values PDF" and you will find multiple lists of things people value. Determine those that most matter to you.)

Afterward, take some time to pray and ask Holy Spirit what needs to be added or taken away so that you are not overwhelmed with so many. There are values specific to your heart that God wants you to know about because they will help you thrive in your identity.

List your values in order from the most valuable to the least and out beside them write a description of what that looks like in your life. For example, peace is a value of mine, so taking my thirty-minute lunch break away from my coworkers is what that looks like for me. It may look like taking an extra ten minutes to stop by a park and just relax before going home because you desire that alone time with yourself.

1. List out ten things you value in your life.
2. Ask Holy Spirit what needed to be added or taken away so that you are not overwhelmed.
3. List them in the order of importance to you, most to least important.
4. List out beside them what that value looks like in your life.

Values list

_____
_____
_____
_____
_____
_____
_____
_____
_____
_____

Most to least important values and what that looks like

_____
_____
_____
_____
_____
_____
_____
_____
_____

Creating Healthy Boundaries

What does it look like to create healthy boundaries? For one, boundaries are meant to allow space for you to create healthy relationships with others, not block them. Many people believe that boundaries are walls that keep people out, but walls are meant to block and separate, not to create healthy relationships. In creating boundaries, I had a hard time even knowing my own boundaries. For me to understand, I really had to dig deep to get to the root causes as to why I did not have them. For instance, I had issues with abandonment and rejection, so I would keep people around longer than they needed to be. I knew it. They knew it also, but they benefited from this situation.

So, a healthy boundary I had to create was to express how important communication and relationships are to me. I expressed how I loved being around those who wanted the best for me. This began a journey to discovering that not everyone wants the best for you. So, it made it somewhat easy to create boundaries around those people.

When I discovered that some people in my life drained me of my time and energy, I placed boundaries as to how long we could talk as well as what we discussed. If it was gossip, I had to learn to shut it down before it started. When it came to them asking my opinion on certain decisions, they had to understand I was not going to go deep with them unless they truly wanted a solution. It was very hard, and at times I wanted to avoid all conversations due to this, but it had to be done.

By setting boundaries, I was able to really enjoy conversations without thinking others will not listen to me or to think they will leave me. I set a time limit and, after that, if I chose to continue, I would express, *Hey, let's continue this conversation.* I gave myself permission and took ownership of the situation. It empowered me to say I had a choice, not to say I did not before, but there was freedom in my boundaries.

As I stated in the beginning of this section, many believe boundaries are walls to keep people out. What that tells me is that it is either your way or no way or there are underlying control issues; trust me, I have been both. That is not how we create healthy, lasting relationships with yourself and others.

We are all created to have relationship with others, and when God is truly in the mix of a relationship, friendship, partnership, etc., it is for your good, not bad. God does hold us accountable for how we steward them, but in the end, He gives us people to help us, be companions or whatever, but He also wants us to play our part and use discernment when people are just flat out using our time, abilities, talent, etc. for their own selfish reasons.

Let's Process

In the space below or in your journal, begin to take inventory of what boundaries you need to begin setting for yourself in your journey. Write the boundary and write why the boundary is needed. We are surprised at what comes up when we truly take the time to think about our decisions.

1. What boundaries do I need to set?

_____
_____
_____
_____
_____
_____
_____
_____
_____

2. Why do I need a boundary in this area?

_____
_____
_____
_____
_____
_____
_____
_____
_____

Creating Daily Habits and Healthy Routines

Once I began seeing how my values, priorities, and healthy boundaries served me in my daily walk of healing and my identity, I had to also address my daily habits and routines. Before healing, my life was in chaos and disorganized. I did not have a set schedule because I was used to getting up and doing. But once I identified my values, I valued my quiet time in the morning with a nice cup of coffee. I usually woke up around five a.m. and would start my day; now I wake up at that time, and I have a moment to sit and think of things outside my daily plan.

As you heal, you realize that things you were doing just to be doing did not serve you well. Getting up at five a.m., rushing to get a shower, gobble down breakfast, and head out for work put me in a place where I was not able to be the best LaRhonda and my routine left me frustrated and upset at myself because I did not take time to care for my needs.

When we wear masks, we usually are going, going, going. We do not have time for ourselves, and we create atmospheres in our bodies where stress and anxiety thrive. We create sickness, strain, and muscle aches and pains that should not be there. We create relationships with our children or loved ones as transactional versus loving and kind. We start a downward spiral into allowing our trauma wounds to grow and create more infection because we are running on E.

In creating a daily routine, you are taking the time to examine what works best for you so that you can show up whole and authentic. Your routine does factor in other priorities you cannot do without, but it is for you to take time to discover how you can function at an optimal level. Daily habits may include a fifteen-minute shower before getting ready for work. It may be spending time with your spouse before cooking breakfast. It may be taking those fifteen minutes to go walking. Does it align with your values and priorities? Does getting in the habit of preparing your meals ahead take stress off your mornings where you may have been rushing to eat breakfast and fix lunch at the same time?

I am going to give you an example of how values, priorities, and boundaries in place may help correct or rid your body of some illnesses we believe are generational or incurable. Many do not know that high stress levels in the body create a hormone called cortisol. Cortisol plays a role in letting the body know it is under stress. Cortisol is active and is pretty much sugar to fuel the body when high stress levels are activated. This type of sugar helps to feed the body when in fight or flight mode.

If cortisol stays in your blood stream for too long, it can cause major conditions such as diabetes, anxiety, and depression. This is also the reason for female reproductive issues such as polycystic ovary syndrome (PCOS) or thyroid issues. The normal functions that serve us in emergencies are void when this process occurs, and our bodies are put into a state of "dis-ease." Disease is nothing more than the body's way of telling us that something is out of order and alignment. Some diseases may be caused from genetics, but the majority are caused by our own doing.

The above example is just one of many ways we can take control back from the medical ailments and mental issues we have. This goes back to identity. When we do not identify and call the thing we are struggling with by its real name, we are not able to overcome it with healing. When we are stuck in blaming others for the way our life has turned out, we do not receive the healing God has promised us.

Take a moment to evaluate the state of your health this week. If there are any underlying conditions you have, list them below, and then list the things your doctor has told you about how to handle them from a nonmedicinal perspective. After you create the list, spend time with Holy Spirit to ask God where you should start. It may be something as simple as drinking more water, not watching TV for a week, taking a five-minute walk outside, or even spending some time in the evening with your children. God is practical and does not give you the answer to the problem without giving you simple instructions.

_____

_____

_____

_____

_____

_____

_____

_____

_____

_____

ISSUES WILL COME UP

Leaving Behind What Doesn't Serve You and God

Take a deep breath. Hold it for five seconds if you can. Breathe.

I wanted you to take this pause because you have come so far and have more than likely become overwhelmed at what you have taken in. I know it can be a lot, and I understand where you are. When change happens, it can be overwhelming because the newness of change is foreign. We have been used to chaos and operating from places of lack and abandonment. We have tried to fix everyone and everything around us. We do not know how to handle silence when it happens and not think the worst of everything. We do not know or understand what it feels like to not have to fix something or someone but accept what and who they are.

In this moment, God is teaching you to be still. In this season, your rest will come when you begin to know and trust God in every part of your life, known and unknown. You will see goodness in every situation because you will have an opportunity to get to know God more intimately. When we begin to trust God in the process and obey His directions, we begin to see radical healing in areas we thought would take years or decades. God is not concerned with time because He does not operate from that space; we do. God is concerned about His will for your life and making sure you are protected and safe during the process.

In this section I want to discuss what leaving behind what doesn't serve God looks like. It is a topic many begin to back away from because they associate it with being lonely. In this season of change and God working with you on your identity, pushing away or stepping back from things that do not serve you will be helpful. I'll give an example for reference.

If you are a gardener or look out at flowers and plants like fruits and vegetables, you see a garden or orchard that is almost flawless. You see the harvest and everything in alignment. But what is unknown to you is how much it took to keep it up. One aspect of gardening is ensuring that weeds do not strangle the plant or fruit. When gardeners and farmers go in, they are making sure weeds are not growing up with the plants. They can easily become entangled and cut off the water or nutrient supply needed to help the plant grow.

When this happens, you think the plant will do well with a few weeds, but later you may see the plant wither and die. This is not what the gardener or farmer wanted for their harvest. So, there are many times they must get down on their knees and pull up those weeds from the roots in order to remove what is not needed in the garden.

This goes for our life as well. Our identity depends on it. As I heal, there is a daily pulling of weeds and roots I must pull out or deal with. This does not mean I do it alone. Whether I share my struggles with my own personal group of women I trust or I begin to journal these things, continuing to address my wounds helps to keep the weeds out my life and off my identity. In the past when I allowed people, places, and things to dictate my life, the weeds of their words and expectations almost choked me and killed me in my prime. I have known God for over twenty years, but I was not tending to the garden He gave me. I allowed people to plant seeds of destruction, confusion, and chaos in my garden to the point where I could not recognize truth when I saw it.

So today, I am intentional and mindful of who speaks to me, as well as the seeds they are planting. I am intentional in what I write because I know the power of words. Even in speaking with others about their own hurts, I do my best to not become so human with them that they feed off my energy and get the notion that it's okay to sin. Because it is not okay to be outside God's will for your life.

It is never okay to willfully sin and believe grace will continue to cover it. Grace does cover our sins, but there comes a time where you must pull out the twins of decisions: accountability and responsibility. If you do not, you will always see yourself as a victim and act as a victim in every situation and wonder why you are still hurting.

Let's Process

So now it is time for you to write out your "weeds" that you have not pulled up in your garden. What weeds are in your life that you know you need to take hold of from the root and pull? Is it unforgiveness, jealousy, self-victimization? These are all weeds used by the enemy to steal, kill, and destroy your garden. By calling it what it is, even down to the exact language, you will have to face it with courage, but you will not have to do it alone. You will have allowed God's love to come and help you dig out the very things that have been trying to overtake you for years.

Weeds I need to pull up

1. What weeds are in your life that you need to pull up from the root?

   _____
   _____
   _____
   _____
   _____

2. Why are the weeds there?

   _____
   _____
   _____

3. What will you replace once the weeds are pulled up?
_____
_____
_____
_____
_____
_____
_____
_____
_____

What is Holy Spirit Saying?

We can hear God, and in this moment, His voice should be the only one that matters. I say this because even in my own healing today, God is still speaking to me. Holy Spirit is my Comforter when I feel afraid. I am being guided to people, places, and resources to solve my issues. I do not walk alone. God is our ultimate resource and all we will ever need, and He uses people like you and me to help others.

Think about this before moving forward in this book. If there is a family in need, who does He usually use in these cases? He uses people like you and me to bless the family. This is not to say God in all His power could not give them groceries from the sky, but remember this: We are the hands and feet of Jesus on earth. We live in a physical realm.

We must have such a bond with our Father that if He tells us to supply a family with one month's rent, we say yes and know God provides and has a storehouse of more awaiting requests. Yes, this has happened before, but God knew before He asked you to do it that you could provide it. This is just a test of your faith, and He gives you free will to choose whether you want to or not.

In the next few chapters, I will discuss the restoration process and how being a good steward, now, will help accelerate your restoration process as well as what God is doing for you in the process.

In the space below, write down what Holy Spirit has spoken to you thus far in the plan you have created for your identity.

Holy Spirit is saying...

_____
_____
_____
_____
_____
_____
_____
_____
_____
_____
_____
_____
_____
_____
_____
_____
_____
_____
_____
_____

Chapter Five
Restoration from False Identity

As I continue in my restoration of who I am in Christ, I have learned some key steps and must-haves that God has shown me are essential. Before I began seeking God for who I am, I assumed it would be a long, hard road. I believed I would be doing this work by myself. When I finally surrendered and allowed the process to take place, I realized God is a god of grace. He truly orchestrated each move—even those moves I was kicking and screaming in—and showed me grace. He knew this work was not easy for me or any one of you. He knows exactly what you have been through and what it cost you to keep it. But He is now wanting you to open your hands and let go. Let go of all the pain and the past hurts, both physically and spiritually.

He wants what is best for you, but He is asking you to uncover the wound so He can see it, even though He knows what it is. He is asking you to admit your faults and worries to Him because when He sends you the person who is ordained and called by Him to help you, He wants you to get used to telling your story and being vulnerable with His chosen people. You will not heal until you reveal the troubles of your heart.

In this chapter we will discuss how gracious God is through our process of healing, as well as giving you a foundation to maintain and keep your identity as God has shown you. God wants you to work with Him because He can show and tell you more than anyone who has ever known you. Even today, God reveals areas of my heart and soul that need to be healed. I have not come to the point of not needing His healing touch. I will say, as I begin to clean out those areas that were cluttered, there is clarity in my behaviors, habits, and right restoration because it is begin sustained with these key tips.

Surrender

Surrender is essential in the very beginning of your healing and restoration. When a doctor places a patient on the table for surgery, the patient is aware that they are surrendering their life over to the surgeon. They must sign a consent that outlines the risks involved in their surrender, including death. God does the same thing for us. For us to be in complete surrender, there is a covenant that is to be made.

Jesus showed us that His life was the signature on the consent. Jesus knew he must lay down his life for the greater good. God knows and shows you that in order to heal these trauma wounds, a surrender and giving over of your life must come first. If you have not given your life over to Christ, you may experience some healing by following these steps, but you will not receive the full blessing God has in store for you by surrendering your life over to Jesus.

The surrender takes place in your heart. Your heart can be deceitful, but it does reveal the troubles you have. Your surrender looks like you are letting go of that son or daughter who does not want to live right or has not accepted Jesus into their life. God knows their choice and God will handle them accordingly, but God needs you to be the light and you can't when you won't let go of the people you love the most. God wants to make you the example of His love and grace, but He must deal with your heart and wounds first.

Our life will need to be in alignment with God, but you cannot come into alignment with something you do not believe. Surrendering your thoughts and religious beliefs is the next to let go. The surrendering of these does not mean you let them go, but that they are shaped back to their original purpose. Being religious is attempting to do good just to go to heaven or be in God's graces. Religion has taught us that we need to do so in order to be saved.

God has already loved us. He is just showing us what it looks like to walk in it. We are not broken individuals. That is what the world tells us daily. But when you surrender to the brokenness the world claims, you tell yourself you must fix it all by yourself. You tell yourself you need crystals, tarot, witch spells, psychics, medication, herbs, drugs, etc. in order to feel whole again.

When we take on the posture of surrender, we tell God in that moment, *Lord, you are my healer, and you are how I am made and how I function*. You let God know you are ready to lay it all at the cross at the feet of Jesus, so that He can take on the sins you once had. And as Jesus has already done, he takes those sins and cast them far away because they are no more, and Jesus has conquered sin just for you.

Laying it at the Cross

There is so much to say when we begin to lay our sins at the cross. Anything that takes our eyes off God or causes us to not look to Him as the source for all our needs leads us into darkness. God is the light and answer to all our situations. Just think. Our God has a solution to each situation we face in life. It just takes us deciding to do it His way regardless of what that may look like. But how hard is it sometimes just to lay it down!

We can look at other's situations and create a beautiful plan for their life. But when it comes to us laying down just one thing, we fuss and fight about it. I know there were times in reading the chapters that called you to release when you had a hard time. I know because I am still laying things at the cross. Some days I feel like I will never stop. But I realize that the more I lay at the cross, the more freedom I experience. It is like doing spring cleaning. We have jam-packed so many things for years in boxes, totes, and bags. We go through it all, and it feels like we will never stop unpacking or throwing away things.

When I moved from the home of my ex-husband, after the divorce was finalized, I realized I carried so much stuff with me for the last seven years, from when I moved to Nashville, our first home, etc. It was just junk that I had not even laid eyes on in a year. I was shocked and disappointment that I allowed it to get to this point. This is how we view our wounds and issues. We have allowed these to pile up in our hearts and do not even have room for others, including God's love. But when asked to release, we hoard them, as though we will die without it. This is not the type of life God wants for his children.

Laying everything at the cross requires a choice. It requires us to truly take inventory and ask God, *What do I need to lay down?* I still have conversations with God about memories, heartaches, things that give me headaches, and materialistic things that I just want to hold on to. I realize when I get to that point where I am holding on, that I am holding on to something I assumed was part of my identity, and I gone back into thinking that without this thing I am no one. That is how the enemy can creep in and stall your healing process.

It is so essential to take inventory of all the things we hold near and dear, including our children. Yes! Our precious children. We should not be holding onto their responsibilities when they make choices they have been educated on. I say that because for years, my son, although a Christian, made choices that were not good for him and later suffered the consequences for them.

There were many times I saved him from his consequences, but one day God spoke to me that I was doing what my mother did to my father and brothers, saving them from their clearly decided choices. She worried all the time, and I remember telling myself that I would not do that to my own. Years later, I found myself doing such and becoming so sick, but at the same time addicted to the cycles. I had to lay it all at the cross, including the root of it, which was the example seen by my mother.

Obedience

I never realized how much power and authority were given to me when I walked in obedience. It did not mean I did not mess up or fall, but it meant that the minute I realized I was not in God's will, or I knew I was not in His presence anymore, I repented and turned back. I have so many examples when doing things in my own will led me further away from God. But I have even more examples when I walked according to what God said.

My main example is something that is present, and I am still in awe about. Before letting my ex-husband know I wanted a divorce, I had been praying to God for a better way. I was exhausted and not aware of what to do next. God reminded me, *You have a choice, and with those choices are different roads. I am with you either way, but just know there is a choice to be made.* I had heard this the previous year, but it meant more this time around. But in that choice, I must do what God says and move accordingly.

For a long time, I felt my marriage was not out of right love but a desire to not be in sin. Yes, there was obedience there, but if I had taken the time to truly seek God and know who I am, we would have remained friends. The marriage was not done in obedience. So, when I made the choice, I felt a weight be removed.

I felt a spiritual change happen in me and in the home until I left. There was an unmasking of what had been there all along but I could not see. I was able to truly hear and desire to hear

God more, as well as know when His voice was speaking. I realized after that day, I had the choice to walk in obedience according to God's will or go my own way and do as the world tells women who are open, walking wounds. I chose to go inside myself and seek help from a therapist and coach. By doing that and doing as God instructed me to do, even though it was very hard, my obedience was the key to my peace and freedom.

When you walk in obedience in your healing journey, you are protecting yourself from the enemy and the "little foxes" that get in the way of moving forward. Men can easily fall into that trap of sleeping with a lot of women and never committing again, but it is obedience to God, and knowing that a person's choice is not your validation of who you really are, that keeps you closer to God and the enemy off your back. As women, it is easy to fall into the role of independent woman and never allow a man to come in, but through obedience we become humble and closer to God, depending on Him to supply our needs and protect us from hurt through His holy instruction.

Last, obedience is the key to winning your battles, seeing your wounds healed, and bringing restoration to yourself and those after you. The perfect example of disobedience is in the book of Jonah when God told Jonah to go to Nineveh to prophesy to the people about their behaviors and lifestyle.

Jonah intentionally ignored God, not just because he didn't want to go, but the root was the history with the people he was being sent to speak to. Not only did his disobedience affect him but those that were in the boat with him, which almost killed them. When Jonah realized the storm was God's doing, he asked them to throw him off the boat. Once that happened, he was swallowed by a whale.

God's protection for his child came in the form of a response of Jonah's obedience. Can you see how your disobedience can place others in jeopardy? Make sure today you follow obedience despite how you may feel. Your obedience is the key to healing all areas in your life and your family.

Creativity is Key

This is the fun part of your journey. This is where you get to place your own spin on how you will heal and how you will conquer those things that had you bound. As I was healing and even to this day, I have found joy again in doing those small things I stopped. For example, I love to use colors and just draw or paint. So, one day I was wanting to do this, and I went out and bought paint, markers, crayons, etc.

If you saw me, you would have thought I was a teacher buying supplies for school. I got home and began coloring and painting. After completing my project, I felt so relived. It was the outlet I needed to get my emotions, frustrations, and feelings out. Being creative can look like a variety of things. God does not place us in a box; we do.

There is something about being in a creative space that releases solutions to our problems. Some may like to do pottery, dance, sing, write, journal, walk, garden, etc. In just that list of activities, it helps us create an atmosphere where God is easily visible to us. It helps us to usher in His presence in a way we may not even think to experience. I was told many times to not hold back where I was being led when I needed a release or outlet to channel my thoughts or emotions. My default always took me to writing, but there was a period in my life where I could not write.

Through healing, I was able to pick up the pen again and create from a space where I was currently with my emotions, thankfulness, and overall freedom. When I let go of the need to suppress or depress my feelings, I was able to write whatever I wanted, in freedom, knowing God was leading me to let it go. Yes, I was even trying to censor my own writing.

As silly as it may sound, I did not want to reread or see the hurt I was transcribing on paper. So much pain and hurt were behind my words that I did not believe it all came from me. Going back over some of my tough days in my journals, I saw clearly where I was. There was nothing hidden, and the wound was ugly to see. I saw how my thinking led me to situations that, if I had been healed, it would not have gone that far.

God gave us the ability to create because He is a creator. He does not hold back; He has no limits. Why do we limit this part of us that God has given to us freely? God is wanting you to explore again and be free from the constraints the world places on us as we grow. Did someone tell you it was childish to run or sit in the rain? Did someone tell you to shut up when you made up songs just because? Did someone tell you to stop dancing because you couldn't? Did someone tell you that you are too old to play with dolls? I know there is more examples, but these are just a few. What I am saying is that God created you just as you are—embrace the beauty in those words alone.

Let's Process

Down in the space below or in your journal, write what made you happy while you were being creative, but you stopped because of people, places, things, and ideas of who you need to be got in the way?
Creativity

1. What made you happy while you were creating?

_____
_____
_____

2. What stopped you?

_____
_____
_____

3. How are you creative?

_____
_____
_____

4. How can you add one of these to your daily life?

_____
_____
_____

Always Operate in Truth

When we are operating from a place of sound truth and faith, we can defeat the things that come to break us down and drag us back to brokenness, hurt, pain, breakdowns, suicidal ideations, etc. Truth means the Word that God gave us to stand on when things around us are shaky. The truth spoken in the silence, when no one is around, that God said you are healed but you were to hurt to believe you could be put back together.

When we operate from a place of truth, we walk in authenticity, and no one can take that away from you. Yes, people will walk away from you. Yes, people will look at you strange. Yes, you will feel alone, but you are not alone. You are being healed, and in rehabilitation centers it is mainly you, the doctors, and nurses, as well as physical therapists, who are rehabbing you back to life.

You cannot go into rehab with all those people with you. You must operate in truth and where you truly stand. When you are in rehab, the doctor places an order for all these people to come in and create plans to get you back as close as possible to where you were before you were injured. They come in and talk with you, dig deep into your fears, give medications to keep the pain at bay until you can move without it, and nurse you back to a place where you can walk in confidence and be better and stronger with the tools given.

When they are finished, you are partially finished ... according to your work. I want you to take a minute to think about that. When God is working on us, He is continually doing a work in us, and it is not in our strength. When we try to restore ourselves, we are incomplete because there are things no one can truly give to us. Only God knows what we need, and then God will use someone to execute your prayer. Therefore, leaning in and truly hearing Holy Spirit is so important in your healing journey.

Last, when we operate and walk in truth, we walk in freedom—freedom to do God's work and freedom to just be. When we are walking in obedience, we are yielded and submitted to God's work. When we walk in obedience, we are allowing God to protect us from what we cannot see. In your healing, you will be faced with spiritual warfare because you are using their weapon that they cannot stand against.

God fights the battle, and you just must stand. When you stand in your weakness, God is then able to show you what to operate in His strength looks like. I will leave you with this Scripture from Isaiah 1:19–20 (NKJV): "'If you are willing and obedient, you shall eat the good of the land; but if you resist and rebel, you will be devoured by the sword'; For the mouth of the Lord has spoken."

Will you begin to walk in obedience or continue to do and heal yourself by yourself?

Chapter Six
Being a Good Steward of Your Restoration

You are in the final stretch of the stretch. You have learned that you must allow yourself to let go and forgive yourself in order to start to heal. You have learned that you must get real and honest with yourself in order to know that you need healing. You have learned the steps to take as well as taken notes along the way to pull out those things you never thought were bothering you.

Identifying wounds was a section where things got real. Opening those bandages to reveal the infections that have skewed your vision was powerful. You learned to go to God to seek the answers you need and then walk out the solution Holy Spirit gave you just for you. You learned to operate in your weakness and allow God's strength to show itself mighty in your life.

Despite how tough you may perceive it to be from this point, know that Jesus paid the price. He paid the outcome of the separation we had with God through His obedience. He allowed the veil to be torn and remain torn between us and God. Holy Spirit gives us, straight from heaven, the solutions we need to navigate through this physical realm. We bring heaven to earth when we walk in those solutions because those solutions are testimonies of God's goodness to us that show others He can be trusted.

As we continue to walk out our healing, we need to understand how important it is to also be a good steward of the victory we have been given. As we walk out our solutions, there are things we are going to be doing daily to keep us in this posture of surrendering our life over to Him. Being a steward means taking care of the things, people, ideas, places, etc. that God has given us. Yes, this means our healing is a gift from God and we are to steward it accordingly. Through our healing, we will be the example to others of how God heals us His way, versus the world's way.

Seeking God's Heart Daily

Seeking God daily is a term used when we want to let others know what to do but not how to truly do it. It can be used passively, but for those who are unaware of what that means, here is the definition and example.

When many people in today's world say they are seeking God, they do not define which god they are referring to. They use the phrase passively because it sounds good to say. When I say seeking God, I mean seeking God's heart because it is God's heart for you that sets you free and able to heal. When we are seeking God, we need to realize that seeking means we are looking for God's answers, not our own or the world's way of doing a thing. God's heart shows us that He has our best in mind and in His heart.

You have probably heard the verse, "Love the Lord your God with all your heart, with all your soul, and with all your mind" (Matthew 22:37 nkjv). Many breeze through it and say it passively, but I want to focus for a minute on the goodness of this sentence Jesus spoke. Jesus spoke this after the Pharisees asked *What is the greatest commandment?* There was good reason to speak on this ultimate commandment. Many, including the Pharisees, were seeking God but not His heart. They put God in a box for so many centuries for the sake of seeking and following commands that they forgot to love God.

In seeking God, we must fall in love with God's heart. Not just to follow rules but to become intimate with Him so that when we go to God, we know His heart for the matter. For those who have children, we have grown to know what they need even in how they say something. We know how they want a certain thing even if they do not have the words to explain. We connect with their heart, and we make sure they are good. In a similar sense, when we are seeking God, it is not for us to get what we want. We want what God wants, and that is His best on the matter or situation.

So daily seeking God's heart requires us to have a relationship with Him that is not superficial but intimate. Knowing God's heart takes us from a place of wanting things our way to allowing God to have His way in our life and healing. When we position ourselves daily to seek in this manner, we are more than likely to be obedient to His voice and instructions versus having a struggle. We yield what we want to God, and He gives us more than we could ever imagine—and without the brain power we expend when we are trying to think of things on our own.

Communication and Community is Key

Communication with God should not be a genie-in-a-bottle session. It should not be a time to tell on others and wish for God to throw down fire on all those coming against you. No. Communication is simply a moment you have with God, listening to His heart and asking questions regarding why, how, possibly when, and thanking Him for his goodness to allow you to join in on His plans. This is also called prayer.

Praying to God should be a daily thing like showering or using the bathroom. It is something most people do not realize will set you up for success for that day when you implement it into your daily life. Prayer has been regarded as a confession session or genie-in-a-bottle session. But let's take a deeper look into prayer. When I pray, I come seeking His wisdom and understanding on a matter, as well as forgiveness. If there are needs, I will ask strategically. I do not come to God telling Him to fix it, but He shows me where or who I may go to for the help. In my moment of prayer, I am sitting with Him and being patient, waiting on what He wants to tell or show me.

Prayer is also my petition. I can petition God on something He has already told me and ask what I need to do or ask for patience or whatever the case may be. How does this relate to identity restoration? Everything. Going to God to consult with Him about your identity helps you to not only know His heart for you personally but to open those layers in a way that no one else can open. Prayer creates a space of protection, intimacy, and vulnerability and allows Holy Spirit to flow and give simple directions of how to maintain a certain area you need healing in.

God's space at His feet brings clarity once you give the clutter to Him. Praying strategically gives God the position to be your strength in your life when you are weak. Making the choice to pray daily and seek His heart on the matters of your heart bring a goodness you will not experience by taking your issues to anyone who does not even understand or even know your heart.

This brings me to my next point, which is community. Once you have come from a place of chaos or dysfunction, God will place you in a community of people who will support your healing. They will begin to uphold you and encourage you to follow in the ways of our Father and not allow negative thoughts from you or anyone to cut open healed wounds. We can easily get into a situation where we believe we can go out into the world again and do it the same way. No. God has done a new thing when you began to walk in your rightful identity. You cannot go the same places and be the same person you were before healing. You cannot do the same things you once did.

When you are in a safe community, you can be challenged without condemnation. You are given different things to work on and you have people in there who are currently doing the work of healing and have been able to keep their healing and are living it daily. Being in communities that have no God-given solutions or focus will not be beneficial. It may feel good and place similar people around you, but if no one is seeking God's heart when you have questions or situations, it is time to leave.

Sharing Your Journey

In creating this book with God, I realized how powerful my testimony of healing will be to others. Even the pieces of myself I share on social media and what I share behind closed doors do set others free. They can see pieces of themselves in me, and that is truly something I am thankful for daily. When you begin to share your journey, you will see yourself in others when they begin to share. You will see where they are and think, *Man, I was there at one point and know exactly how they are feeling.*

Your experience was not meant to be placed under a rug or in a journal and closed shut. We are all changed by testimonies. Whether they are to keep going or keep seeking God, our lives serves a purpose. God has placed us on this earth for relationships, and there is power in agreement. If you think about the most influential people, whether an artist or actor, when they share their beginnings, people can relate and see themselves in that situation. Usually, others become inspired by their strength to get going in the face of adversity. Instead of us going in our own strength, we testify to God's strength and power in our life through our act of surrender and faith.

As you heal, begin to tell others. You do not have to be completely healed but come from a place where you do not struggle with that thing or have at least mastered over it with instructions from Holy Spirit. There is nothing more discouraging than being on the fence talking about healing and then in the same sentence telling others God didn't heal you.

People will begin to see and hear our testimony and discover and experience God in a different way. Nothing is more powerful than seeing miracles in other people's lives, whether it be through healing, getting off drugs, surviving abuse, etc. When we testify to the goodness of God, we open doors for people who may not have come to God if it was not for us speaking up and sharing. There is so much power in your share. We share the gospel of Jesus when we share our testimony.

Live Out Your Journey Fearlessly

You are now in a place of no return. If you return to your old ways, or open your healed wounds, you will have made the choice to return to a place of death. This may sound harsh, but from experiencing the light, only to turn around and almost die, I refuse to go backward. You must make that your final answer. Turning back to your old way doesn't even serve you. At the best, you experience double pain and trouble.

Have you ever seen someone cut open a healed wound because there was infection that was unseen due to not caring for it? Have you ever seen someone re-break a bone because it healed wrong? These moments are painful, and I have had to watch them go through the pain of healing all over again, but it saved their life. Now, I am not saying you will be perfect in your journey, but I am stating, do not allow anyone or anything to take your victory. Do not allow the enemy to reclaim your healing. This is called fear or sabotaging yourself.

When we walk out our healing fearlessly, we tell others that we walk with God and we are not alone in this. From the beginning, I have stated that the difference in healing yourself and allowing God to come in, is that you will never do it alone. You will always have a God there with you during the hardest moments. Walking fearlessly simply means: I recognize the fear that comes with this new area, but I will not yield to fear. I will surrender to God. I will continue to walk by faith even when I do not understand the outcome of it all.

Living out this new life in Christ will come with some fear, especially when the world is against you. But in the walk, you do not walk alone. I cannot stress this enough. For years I felt like I was walking alone with my pain. I thought this was what life was and I did not see a way out from the burdens and pressures of others to carry loads that were not mine. But then I caught the revelation from my mentor who had overcome what I was walking in and was living her life according to what God was telling her versus what she was telling herself.

I saw the example and heard the testimony, and I thought surely if God can do that for her, He will do it for me. It was that faith that had me write this book. It was that faith that helped me heal. God is continuing to help me live out this journey fearlessly, with community and Holy Spirit, and I am forever grateful to be in this space, season, and time with you all to share my story and wisdom as well. So, walk this journey out fearlessly and may the Lord continue to bless you on this new journey to healing.

> Therefore, I remind you to rekindle the gift of God that is in you through the laying on of my hands. For God has not given us a spirit of fear, but one of power, love, and sound judgment. So don't be ashamed of the testimony about our Lord, or of me his prisoner. Instead, share in suffering for the gospel, relying on the power of God. (2 Timothy 1:6–8 CSB)

Chapter Seven
What God Does for You in Recovering Your Right Identity

As you begin to see the fruits of your healing, remember that God wants the best for you. God will not half-step on the promises. In my own life, God has done these things I am going to mention. Through obedience and really walking out my right identity, I have been able to overcome my past and move into the future God has for me. This doesn't mean I did not go through suffering or pain. I went through it all, because I knew God would be glorified. Healing through the pain of twenty plus years of unhealed trauma and people pleasing made me realized how powerful Jesus's death on the cross truly meant for me and others who will heal.

The promises I have received through 1 Peter 5:10 (ESV) bring joy and light to my heart: "And after you have suffered a little while, the God of all grace, who has called you to his eternal glory in Christ, will himself restore, confirm, strengthen, and establish you." I have heard this verse for a long time, but it did not become real to me until the last two years. I was asking God, *What would happen if I healed? What would become of me when I really do this healing with you?* And so, by looking at each individual phrase, I could see what He was doing. Here is how God will make new all things in your life through His promises in this verse.

God Will Restore You

God will restore you back to His identity He intended for you to have. It doesn't take long to begin healing once you make the decision that you will obey God in the things He is asking you to do. Holy Spirit empowers you to make those changes and teaches you what to do, where to go, and who to speak to regarding those things that need change. You are not alone.

God begins to take those things that do not belong to you and burn them up. As you begin to walk in obedience, there is almost a new sense of well-being and joy added. You can reverence God more and feel a sense of freedom. The choices you make are no longer for survival but for you to thrive in all areas of your life. You experience the mercy and grace and begin to mature in God versus trying to manipulate God into doing things your way.

There will be a difference in your posture both with God and the people in your life. You will not need to seek validation outside of Him, unless you choose to. God restores relationships that you were unable to mend by your own effort. God will be able to come in and use you as a light to them versus just wanting you around to keep company. The exchanges that will take place will be beyond your understanding, and it will seem there is no effort in this restoration. This is an awesome feeling and experience, so embrace it when you see it.

God Will Confirm You

Since I was eleven years old, I wanted to be confirmed, or given approval, and known by my parents. I wanted them to see me as I am and not my behaviors or reactions. When I came to know God more and decided to do things his way, I realized that He did not condemn me or tell me that I waited too late. He decided to take me as I am and confirm who I am. He reminded me of how much He loved and cared for me. He reminded me of how beautiful He made me. He also reminded me that He is my protector against anything the enemy tries to throw at me. God confirmed me as His daughter by how he nurtured me back to my right mind and rightful place.

Not once did I sense fear or condemnation due to me going back and forth from the enemy's camp when I did wrong. God reminded me that He would fight my battles and He would reassure me of my position, such as what to say and do, by way of Holy Spirit. He never left me nor forsook me, even in my darkest moments. When I wanted to give up on myself because the pain was too much to handle, He strengthened my spirit to keep moving in healing and not to stop.

This is how God confirms you, and this is how He wants us to walk when we feel as though we cannot move forward. He wants us to come to Him. When the world seems to dismiss us due to things we cannot change about ourselves, such as disabilities, economic status, or even our skin color, God confirms us and lets us know who we truly are in Him.

God Will Strengthen You

When I was weak in my sins and could not seem to catch a break from the habitual cycles of hurt, pain, unforgiveness, and resentment, I eventually had to surrender. Through the help of my mentor and friends God placed around me, I was able to gain strength in being obedient. This strength came with power because I was being obedient and doing the work God told me. Holy Spirit showed me strategies and the necessary people and places I needed to go to, because this battle was won. I could not take this on my own.

For instance, my addiction to sex was due to being molested at a young age. I did not know that was the root until I started therapy as well as soul care. As I began to heal, I realized that sex was a tool the enemy used to make me feel less than; therefore, sex was a drug to be used to cover my pain. My pain was because I could not get over my past or understand why I was the target. It was painful to go through the moments of my molestation but more painful that I was never the same after it.

I craved sex because it seemed to be the only tool to suppress my issues I could not deal with. I saw sex as an outlet from my reality. Through sex I felt powerful because I assumed I could use sex to control my situations. As an adult, I realized sex kept me trapped and vulnerable to any attack. When I was tired of sex and tired of the games played using sex, I surrendered trying to control my life and others through sex.

But I was forced to fight due to this surrender. Once I no longer allowed my body to have sex, it craved it even more, and I prayed to God to release the urges. I kept praying and asking, but it was not until I realized this was a choice I was making, and my body was not on autopilot. I had a decision to make, and it would be a radical one. I told myself that if I truly believe God for my healing, I will need to hear every command He gives clearly—and not doubt. This also required ridding myself of the people and places I used to go to because I could no longer be influenced by them. It was very tough, especially after a marriage, but I can say it was worth it.

God truly strengthened me because I made the decision to listen and implement what He asked me to do. Yes, there were some tough days, but I truly know that God was there to strengthen me when I made the choice to save my body for the one man God has for me.

God's strength was truly made perfect in my weakness. I was weak, but God stepped in when I could no longer hold on and wanted to stop the pain. He truly was able to deal with my past during this time, and without sex I had to feel all the hurt, but not alone. Just as a father protects his children, I felt covered, protected, and not alone in my process, and till today, I am still sitting under His covering and never leaving again.

God Will [Re]Establish You

Last, God will re-establish you to your rightful place. While healing me, God removed a lot of people, places, and things in my life. I was hurt but knew it needed to happen. When that took place, God reminded me that He will give me a new foundation, new protection, and a new home. I assumed that I would sit and remain in my home state until my last breath, but as I write this, I will relocate to Texas in the year 2022.

I never saw my home in another state, but I knew eventually God would uproot me and transplant me in a place where I could finally call it home. All my life, I just wanted a solid place to call home, and despite moving from my hometown and relocating to Nashville, Tennessee, I knew it was not the place I would settle. I now can see why because He reminded me that my new place and home were elsewhere and the home I would live in would not have been built.

When hearing this and going through all the pain healing as an adult, I thought time was lost. I did not know I was going to be given a brand-new life. I did not know God wanted to establish a new foundation all together. This is how our Father loves on us and wants us to let go of all the things we accumulated in our own power. He has more in store for us, when we release. God wants to re-establish you.

God wants to re-establish the foundations that were unfinished, broken, or never created in your life. He wants to be the strong foundation you can trust will never give way or crumble. He wants to show you how much you are loved, but you must release the pain and hurt you refuse to deal with. God cannot produce good fruit through you if you do not deal with the bad roots and weeds that crowd your life.

We really want what God has for us, but we are afraid that we will lose who we are that got us here. That version of you served its purpose, but now it is time to upgrade. God wants to give you a new heart that is like Jesus and show you the right ways of the kingdom. He wants to love on you and show you that His love is everlasting, always there to hold you up when you are weak. Let's take Him up on His offer to walk His path versus our old one. God truly adores His children, and Jesus, as the living sacrifice, showed us what it means to be fully loved and fully protected by the blood.

What is Holy Spirit speaking to you about your new and Right Identity in Christ?

Resources

As this book ends, I want to leave you with resources that will be helpful, especially since this book brings up old wounds and new wounds that need caring for in a more professional way. These resources are ones you can look up via your favorite search engine. They are generic search terms due to the nature of websites not always remaining stable or other excellent sites being developed. However, I have tried to supply a current site with each heading. If you are not online or comfortable with a web search (perhaps you are in a situation where it is unsafe for you to leave an online search record), you can just go to your primary care doctor to talk about options that are available in your area. Area librarians can also help you find similar information.

Remember, this journey is not one for you to walk alone but for you to experience the journey of healing and embracing your identity in Christ. I love you all very much and I am praying for all those that take the time to read.

Mental Health and Substance Abuse Hotline and Resources

Suicide Prevention Hotline 1-800-273-8255
https://suicidepreventionlifeline.org/

Suicide Prevention Lifeline
https://www.nimh.nih.gov/health/topics/suicide-prevention

Substance Abuse and Mental Health Services Administration (SAMHSA)
https://www.samhsa.gov/find-help/national-helpline

National Alliance on Mental Health
(This site contains many links to different mental illness services and how to locate them in your area.)
https://www.nami.org/Support-Education/NAMI-HelpLine/Top-HelpLine-Resources

MentalHealth.Gov
https://www.mentalhealth.gov/get-help/immediate-help

Veteran's Crisis Line
https://www.veteranscrisisline.net/

National Domestic Violence Hotline
https://www.thehotline.org/

USDA National Hunger Hotline
https://www.fns.usda.gov/partnerships/national-hunger-clearinghouse

Better Help online therapy (low-cost therapy for those paying out of pocket)
https://www.betterhelp.com/

www.ingramcontent.com/pod-product-compliance
Lightning Source LLC
Chambersburg PA
CBHW061803070526
44586CB00023B/2689